# SHOW-ME-HOW
# I Can Experiment

## Fun-to-do simple science projects for young children

## STEVE & JANE PARKER

SMITHMARK

This edition first published in 1996 by
SMITHMARK Publishers
a division of
U.S. Media Holdings, Inc.
16 East 32nd Street
New York, NY 10016

SMITHMARK books are available for bulk purchase
for sales promotion and premium use. For details
write or call the manager of special sales,
SMITHMARK Publishers, 16 East 32nd Street,
New York, NY 10016; (212) 532-6600.

ISBN 0-8317-7263-8

Publisher: Joanna Lorenz
Project Editor: Judith Simons
Designer: Michael R. Carter
Photographer: John Freeman
Stylist: Thomasina Smith

Printed in China

**PLEASE NOTE**
**The level of adult supervision needed will**
**depend on the ability and age of the**
**child following the experiments. However,**
**we advise that adult supervision is always**
**preferable and vital if the experiment calls**
**for the use of sharp knives or other objects.**
**See the ⚠ symbol for more information on**
**where adult help is needed for each experiment.**

ACKNOWLEDGEMENTS
The publishers would like to thank the following
children who were such wonderful models, and of
course their parents: Dean Denning, Liam and
Lorenzo Green, Kirsty and Rebecca Fraser, Otis
and Alex Lindblom-Smith, Gabriella and Izabella
Malewska, and Antonino Sipiano.

# Contents

# Introduction

Children are very curious people; so are scientists. Both ask questions about the world around them. How does this work? What does that do? Why do things happen? And can things be improved? You may already ask grownups how things happen. What, where, when and why? This means you are already a natural scientist. Scientists find the answers to their questions by doing experiments. You can do the same. This book shows you how to do tests and experiments for yourself. Then you can find

*Find out why some things float and others sink.*

out the answers to your questions like a real scientist. You can also go on to invent more experiments and do more projects. Perhaps you will make a great discovery and become famous!

## Young Scientists

You have already been doing experiments for years, probably without knowing it. When you were a tiny baby, you started to move your arms and legs about. You grabbed and kicked things,

*Make a sound gun with a cardboard tube and discover how sound travels.*

to see what would happen. When you were bigger, you probably did experiments when you played with your toys. Could you eat them? Did they make a noise when you dropped them? Could you pull them apart to see inside? Playing is experimenting, and playing is fun, so experimenting is fun, too.

*Find out why things look backward in a mirror.*

As you do the experiments in this book, you will find out about light and electricity, how water and wind work, and how heat and cold affect things. This book tells you what to do and then explains what happens. All these experiments are safe with the help of grownups. You can also make up your own experiments and find things out for yourself. This way, you will learn more about the world.

## Different Kinds of Science

Science is so huge that no one can know everything about it.

So scientists usually specialize. This means they study just one or a few subjects. For example, medical scientists study why people get sick, and how to make them better. Biologists study animals and plants, where they live and how they grow. Chemists study chemicals and other substances, what they are made of, and how they can be changed and used. Physicists study how things move, what holds them together or pulls them apart, and how energy makes things happen. Astronomers study the planets, stars, the sun and moon, and the whole universe.

## How to Do an Experiment

Whatever scientists study, they usually work in the same way. This is called the scientific method. They do not rush, and they always keep things clean and safe.

• First, the scientist finds out as much as possible about the subject. This is called research. What is already known about the subject? What experiments have other scientists done, and what did they discover? Do people really know the facts, or are they just guessing?

Then the scientist decides on a good question to ask. It should be a new question that no one has asked before. But it must not be too complicated. Most scientists find out more by working in small stages, bit by bit.

The scientist may have an idea of the possible answer to the question. In other words, he or she may guess what will happen in the experiment. This possible answer to the question is called a theory.

Next, the scientist thinks of an experiment that will test the theory to find the answer to the question. This is called planning or designing the experiment. In a good experiment, everything happens clearly and safely, and nothing can go wrong – hopefully!

Now, the scientist gathers all the bits and pieces to do the experiment. These are called the materials and equipment. Everything is set out neatly and cleanly, and labeled clearly, so that there are no mix-ups.

At last, the scientist carries out the experiment, working carefully and safely. He or she finds out what happens by looking and listening, and perhaps, by feeling or smelling. The things that happen are called the results. These are written down carefully in the Science Record Book. Everything is cleaned up and put away afterward.

• Next, the scientist thinks about the results. Were they expected, or not? Is the theory right, or wrong? If the theory is right, the scientist has found something new. If the theory is wrong, the scientist can try to think of another theory, or perhaps, the experiment did not work properly. Remember, no experiment is a failure. A good scientist can always learn from the results, whatever they are.

• After more experiments, the scientist will be able to gather the answers together. He or she must check everything, then check it again. Finally, the scientist may make a new discovery and become famous.

## Being a Good Scientist

Scientists are very careful people. They have to be. They often work with dangerous machines, equipment and chemicals. And science can be very costly. So scientists also need to be sure that their experiments are worthwhile, and that there will be no mistakes. So they make sure everything is thought out and prepared carefully.

When you do experiments, get the materials and equipment ready first. Have a clean, safe area where you do your experiments, as described over the page. And ask a grown-up to check that everything is safe.

*Use a pitcher and a funnel when pouring liquids.*

*Never touch electric sockets, plugs or wires.*

Water is great fun to splash around, as long as you are working in a waterproof area.
*Science tip* For experiments with water or other liquids, see if you can do them in a large bowl, such as a mixing bowl. This catches any splashes or spills.

Heat can be very dangerous. Hot water and steam can burn or scald your skin. And when very hot water is poured into cold jars, beakers or bowls, it can make them crack or melt. So *always* get a grown-up to help you with experiments that need hot water and make sure your equipment can stand up to it. Cookers and kettles must only be used when a grown-up is present. Liquids can boil over suddenly, and things may catch fire without warning.

*Wear a pair of rubber gloves when handling vinegar or lemon juice.*

*Always ask a grown-up to cut anything with sharp scissors or a craft knife.*

*Science tip* Put a metal teaspoon into a jar before pouring in hot water. This should stop the heat from cracking the jar.

Ice can freeze skin just as badly as hot water can burn. Ice has the added danger that it sticks to dry skin. When you make ice in a freezer, get a grown-up to help you.
*Science tip* Use rubber or dishwashing gloves when handling ice. Wet the ice and the gloves first, so they do not stick together.

Electricity from a small battery is usually safe, since there is not enough power to give a shock. Static electricity can sometimes be felt as a tingle that makes you jump. For example, when it builds up on a car and you touch the handle. But the static that builds up on a balloon, as shown in this book, is too small to feel.
*Science tip* The electricity that is used in the home is very dangerous. It can kill! NEVER touch electric sockets, plugs or wires.

Chemicals used in this book are mostly substances used for cooking, and they are harmless in normal quantities. But

*Put a metal teaspoon into a jar before pouring in hot water.*

ood scientists know that chemicals can be dangerous if
hey get into the wrong place. This includes near too much
eat or inside your body if you swallow them. Never taste or
at chemicals that you are using for experiments. Always
sk a grown-up to get the things you need from the
itchen cabinet. *Never* touch cleaning chemicals, medicines
r alcohol.

*Science tip* Use rubber gloves to handle large quantities of
cids like vinegar or lemon juice.

**Cutting** and making holes can be quite difficult. Scissors
nd sharp points can be dangerous if they are not used
roperly. So ask a grown-up to help.

*Science tip* Draw a line where you are going to cut with
cissors, before you start cutting. It is usually easier to follow
 drawn line.

**Label everything.** It is the sign of a good scientist.
our experiment might be ruined if you cannot remember
hat you put in each jar or if you get your chemicals mixed
p. Write labels on pieces of paper or use special sticky-
acked labels. Stick these in the right place, or put them
nder jars or beakers.

*Science tip* Use a pencil for your labels. Some felt-tipped
ens can blot and run if splashed with water.

## Your Science Record Book

All scientists record their experiments and the results. You
need to know exactly what you did during an experiment so
that you can repeat it to check the result or change it to find
out something else. Each time you do an experiment, record
the following information in your book. If you find writing
difficult, ask a grown-up to help with some of the details and
draw a picture of what happened, instead.

- the day and date
- the experiment's name and the idea behind it
- how you did your experiment, perhaps with a drawing
or diagram
- the results, written in words, or perhaps as a chart with
check marks and crosses

You can make a Science Record Book by covering a
notebook or school-type exercise book with colored paper.
The paper needs to be about $1\frac{1}{4}-1\frac{1}{2}$ in larger all around
than the book when it is opened flat.

## Further Research

When scientists have finished their set of experiments, they
often try to find out a little more, perhaps by changing the
experiment slightly. See if you can make changes to some of
your experiments to find out more. Record what you do and
your results in your Science Record Book.

## Your Science Record Book

1 Place the book centered on the
colored paper, with one cover
pen. Turn the edges of the paper over
he cover, and paste them down with
lue. You can snip the corners of the
aper to give a neater finish. Repeat
with the other cover.

2 Decorate the cover with something
scientific, perhaps numbers,
drawings of test-tubes and scientific
equipment, or cutout photographs of
scientific gadgets.

3 Record all the information that
you have learned from your
experiments. If you like, you can stick
some of the things you have made in
the book, to keep.

## Where to Do Experiments

Many scientists work in special rooms called laboratories. There, they have all the equipment, materials, tools and machines they need to do their experiments. But not all science happens in laboratories. To do research, many scientists go to libraries to read books. They visit exhibitions and museums to find out more. They also meet other scientists and talk about their work.

## The Home Laboratory

You can set up your own laboratory in your home or school. It might be in a kitchen, bathroom, shed or garage. You usually need somewhere with waterproof surfaces, where there is no danger of damaging furniture or carpets. Ask a grown-up to choose the best place.

The main thing you will need is a large work surface, like a table. The place should be brightly lit and not too hot or cold. For some experiments, you will need a freezer or a refrigerator with a freezing compartment. You will sometimes need lots of water. Warm water can come from a faucet or a kettle. You might also need somewhere to heat up a saucepan. Always ask a grown-up to help.
*Science tip* Cover your work surface with several layers of old newspaper. This stops paint and food coloring from staining the work surface and will also absorb spilled liquids and glue.

## Materials and Equipment

You will find most of the materials, equipment and tools that you need for your experiments around the house. Always gather everything you need, and check it before you start the experiment. If you do not, you may run out of something halfway through.

If necessary, you can buy extra supplies of pencils, pens, scissors, sticky tape, paper, cardboard, blotting paper, glue, sticky labels and shapes, poster paints and similar things from a good stationery store or office suppliers.

You can find food colorings, baking soda, vinegar, lemon juice, milk, spoons, toothpicks, skewers and similar things in the kitchen.

Batteries, wires and small flashlight bulbs are sold in hardware stores or hobby shops. You can buy small mirrors from a drugstore and sand or gravel from a home-improvement store.

## Be a Green Scientist

Good scientists know that they must look after our planet by saving resources, recycling things and not damaging the environment or causing waste and pollution. This is called being "green" since it helps to save trees, plants, flowers, animals and natural places on our planet Earth.

You can be a "green scientist" by saving, reusing and recycling things. You will also save money!

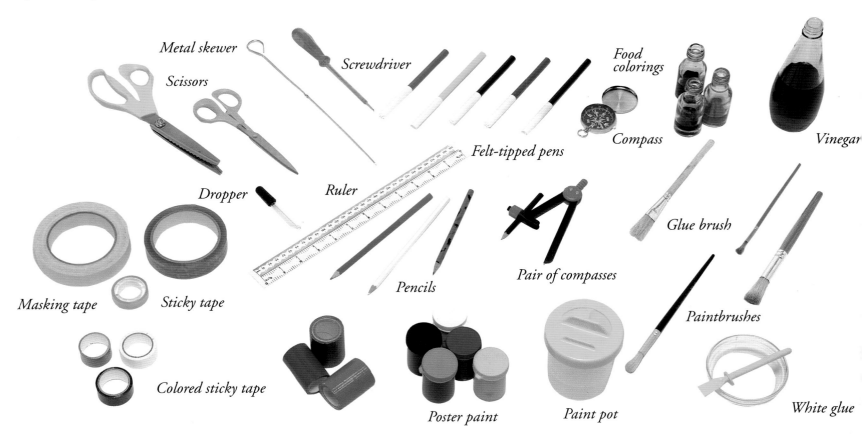

Metal skewer

Scissors

Screwdriver

Food colorings

Compass

Vinegar

Felt-tipped pens

Dropper

Ruler

Glue brush

Masking tape

Sticky tape

Pencils

Pair of compasses

Paintbrushes

Colored sticky tape

Poster paint

Paint pot

White glue

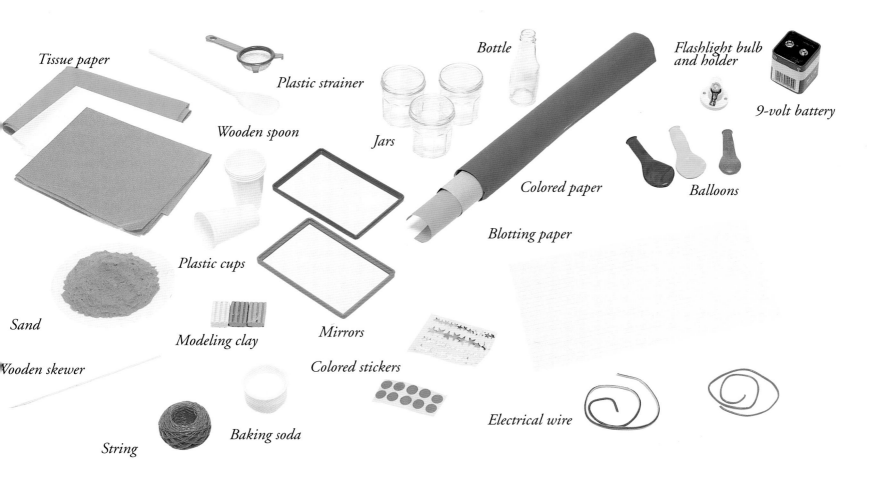

Tissue paper

Plastic strainer

Wooden spoon

Jars

Bottle

Colored paper

Blotting paper

Flashlight bulb
and holder

9-volt battery

Balloons

Plastic cups

Sand

Modeling clay

Mirrors

Wooden skewer

Colored stickers

String

Baking soda

Electrical wire

Use old newspapers, and store your equipment in empty cartons or boxes.

The cardboard from cereal boxes is ideal for experiments.

Ask grown-ups for used paper that has been written on one side. You can use the blank side.

After picnics and parties, wash the paper or plastic cups and plates. You can use them for your experiments.

Save the cardboard tubes from the insides of toilet-tissue rolls and paper towel rolls.

Wash and keep empty jars for your experiments. But remember that glass is easily broken and is then very dangerous to handle.

Save plastic soda bottles. Carefully cut off the tops and turn them upside down to make funnels. The lower parts make plastic jars which are safer than glass ones.

When you have finished with your equipment, take it to your local recycling center.

## Have Fun

If you follow the safety rules in this book and carry out your experiments slowly and sensibly, you will find that science is fun. You can make some amazing discoveries and learn a lot.

Find out more by doing further research, by reading about science, and by watching science programs. You can become an expert scientist and answer all your friends' questions. You might even make a discovery or invention that will change the world!

## A Note for Grown-ups

Some of the experiments in this book can be followed by a child alone, but often adult help is needed. Always supervise your children closely whenever they are using home experiment materials. The places in the book where your assistance is vital, such as when sharp scissors or a craft knife are needed, are marked ⚠.

# Creatures of the Night

Light is bright, and when there is no light, it is dark. A shadow is a patch of darkness. It is formed when something gets in the way of light beams, which can only travel in straight lines. In Alex's puppet show, some of the light from the flashlight shines on the wall. But the light that hits the ghostly black creatures cannot get through or around them. So the wall behind their shapes stays dark and becomes their shady, scary shadows.

You can make the shadows on the wall bigger or smaller. When the puppets are near the torch, they cover more of the light beam, and so the shadows on the wall are bigger, but their edges are fuzzy and blurred.

## Light fantastic

Light is amazing. It comes and goes in a flash, weighs nothing, travels faster than anything else in the universe, and even scientists do not fully understand it. The light we turn on in our homes is produced by electricity. This passes through the very thin wire inside a light bulb and makes the wire glow brightly. The light beams then spread out in all directions and always in straight lines. The light bulb in a torch has a mirror behind it to make all the light beams come out at the front only.

❗ Young children will need help cutting out cardboard shapes with scissors and should not be allowed to handle craft knives. They might also need help in the "dark room," to hold the torch or just for company. Be sure they cannot get themselves locked in a dark room or closet.

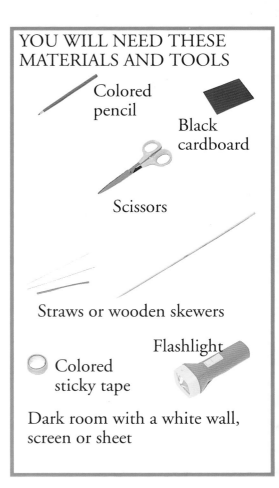

YOU WILL NEED THESE MATERIALS AND TOOLS

Colored pencil

Black cardboard

Scissors

Straws or wooden skewers

Colored sticky tape

Flashlight

Dark room with a white wall, screen or sheet

1 Draw the outlines of some night-time creatures, like bats, owls and spiders, on the black cardboard with the pencil. Make them big.

2 Draw some stars and a moon, too. Cut out the shapes carefully with scissors. If the scissors are sharp, ask a grown-up to help you.

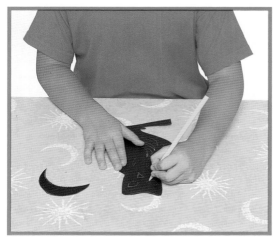

3 Draw features such as eyes and feathers or even bone patterns on to the nighttime creatures. Keep these simple.

## Changing Shadows

Things that light can pass through easily, like air or glass, are called **transparent**. Solid things like your night creature cutouts do not let any light pass through. They are **opaque**. A **translucent** substance is one that lets through some light but not all of it, like tracing paper or tissue paper. Cover one side of a cutout animal with tissue paper. When you hold it up in front of the flashlight, less light will shine through the holes.

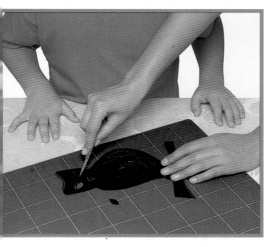

4 Ask a grown-up to cut out the eyes, feather patterns and any other details with a craft knife.

5 Stick the straws or skewers to the shapes with sticky tape to make handles.

6 In a darkened room, ask a friend to shine the flashlight on a light wall. Move the creatures and other shapes in the light to make their ghostly shadows dance on the wall.

# Mysterious Mirrors

Otis is discovering that what you see in a mirror is not an exact copy of the original thing. It is backward – a mirror picture or mirror image. His drawings and writing always look the other way round in the mirror. So does your face! The face that you see when you look in the mirror is a mirror image. It is not the same as the face that your friends and family see when they look at you or when you look at a photograph of yourself.

## Reflections

Light beams travel in straight lines unless they bounce off things. This bouncing is called **reflection**. Only a few things, like the sun, light bulbs, candles and fires, give out their own light beams. These shine into our eyes, and we see them. We see other things because they bounce or reflect light beams into our eyes. Very smooth, shiny surfaces like mirrors are very good at reflecting. When you look at your face in a mirror, you see light beams that have come from the sun or an electric light on your face, bounced off it toward the mirror, and then bounced back again into your eyes!

## YOU WILL NEED THESE MATERIALS AND TOOLS

Paper

Small mirrors

Colored sticky tape

Felt-tipped pens

Otis is having fun making his drawings and writing turn around in a mirror. See if you can make a mirror image come out the right way.

1 Mirrors are made of glass or plastic. Some may have sharp edges. Ask a grown-up to put some sticky tape round them to make them safe.

2 Do a drawing and write what you have drawn on a piece of paper. Be as neat as you can.

3 Hold the mirror up next to the paper. Can you read the writing in it? Does the drawing look exactly the same as it does on the paper?

4 Write the name backward or do the drawing back-to-front. What does it look like in the mirror now?

5 Think of a whole drawing. Draw half of it, using one half of the paper only.

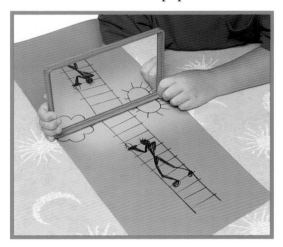

6 Can you make up the rest of the drawing by holding the mirror alongside it? Is the result what you had expected?

## See Back to the Future!

You can make an image bounce backward and forward between mirrors, almost forever. Sit behind one mirror. Hold out another mirror facing you. Look into this mirror. Move both mirrors slightly until you can see the reflection of the mirror in the reflection of the mirror in the reflection of the mirror in the reflection of the mirror and on and on.

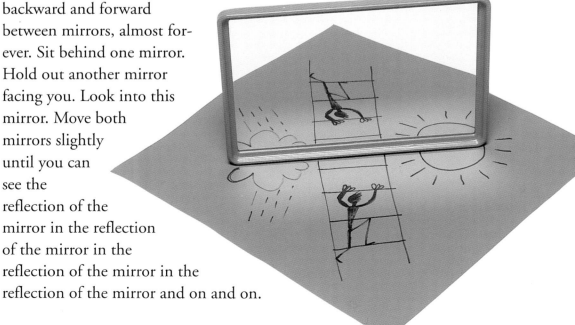

# Tell the Time by the Sun

When the sun rises in the morning, it is low in the sky. It shines on objects from the side to make long, thin shadows. As the sun moves up and across the sky, the shadows get shorter and move around. At midday, the sun is at its highest point, and the shadows are at their shortest. As the sun continues its journey across the sky in the afternoon, the shadows get longer again, but on the other side of the objects.

Gabriella has made a sundial so that she can watch the changing shadow of the dial pointer and tell the time by it.

## Light days and dark nights

Each day, it looks as if the sun moves across the sky. But really, the sun stays still, and it is the Earth that moves. The Earth is like a giant ball that spins around and around. We stay in one place on the surface of the ball, so it looks to us as though the sun is moving. When the sun disappears at night, we are on the shadowy side of the Earth. The sun is still shining, but on the other side. For people there, it i[s] daytime. For us, it is nighttime.

⚠ Young children may need to be shown how to draw a circle with a pair of compasses and how to use a magnetic compass to find north and south. The sundial pointer should face north, since the sun is in the south at midday, so it throws its shadows on to the dial.

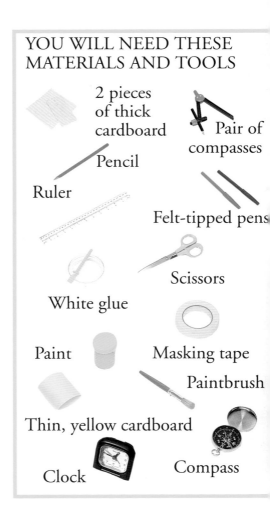

YOU WILL NEED THESE MATERIALS AND TOOLS

2 pieces of thick cardboard

Pair of compasses

Pencil

Ruler

Felt-tipped pens

Scissors

White glue

Paint

Masking tape

Paintbrush

Thin, yellow cardboard

Clock

Compass

1 Open the pair of compasses so the point is about 3 in from the pencil. Push the point into the middle of the thick cardboard, and then turn the compasses to draw a circle.

2 Draw a square on some thick cardboard with a felt-tipped pen and a ruler. Each side of the square should be about 3 in. Draw a diagonal line across the square to make two triangles as shown.

3 Carefully cut out the circle and one triangle from the cardboard. The triangle will be the pointer of the sundial. (You can keep the other triangle as a spare.)

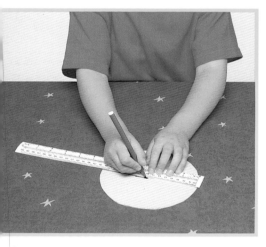

4 Draw a straight line from the center of the circle, where the compass point is, to the edge, using the ruler.

5 Paste the triangle on to the circle along the line using white glue. Hold the triangle in place with masking tape until the glue dries.

6 If you like, paint your sundial bright yellow. Add a smiley face and some wavy sunbeams cut from thin, yellow cardboard.

7 Put your sundial in a safe, sunny place. Find north with the compass. Turn the sundial until the long side of the pointer points toward north. Draw a straight line at the edge of the shadow.

*Right:* You can make your sundial into a clock. Every hour, when the big hand on a real clock gets to 12, draw a line at the edge of the shadow. Write the time by each line.

# Disappearing Rainbow

When sunlight or lamp light shines on a wall, it looks white. But really, it is made up of many different colors – the colors of the rainbow. You can show this in two ways. One is by splitting white light into its different colors with a prism, or you can add the colors together to make white light. Gabriella is doing this by making a colorful spinning top. When she spins the top very fast all the rainbow colors blur and merge together, back into white.

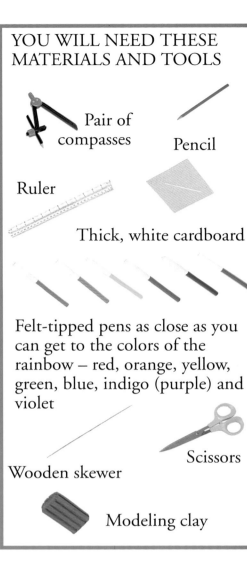

## YOU WILL NEED THESE MATERIALS AND TOOLS

Pair of compasses

Pencil

Ruler

Thick, white cardboard

Felt-tipped pens as close as you can get to the colors of the rainbow – red, orange, yellow, green, blue, indigo (purple) and violet

Scissors

Wooden skewer

Modeling clay

### Rainbows

Rainbows form in the sky when the sun shines on raindrops. The tiny raindrops bend the light beams, separating the different colors. Next time you see a rainbow, look carefully at it. Write down or color in the colors you see in your Science Record Book. These colors are called the spectrum of light. They are always the same and always in the same order.

! Young children may need to be shown how to draw a circle with a pair of compasses and how to divide it into seven equal segments. They may need help with cutting thick cardboard and pushing in the skewer. They may also need help to spin the top fast enough for the colors to merge.

Gabriella can spin her rainbow spinning top to see how the colored light beams blur together and mix into white light.

1 Open the pair of compasses so there is about 2 in between the point and the pencil. Push the point into the center of the cardboard, and draw a circle.

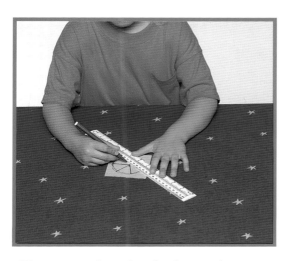

2 You need to divide the circle into seven equal parts, like cutting a cake into seven equal slices. Using a ruler, draw seven lines with a pen or pencil, from the center of the circle to the edge.

3 Carefully cut around the circle with the scissors to make a disc. If the cardboard is very thick, ask a grown-up to help.

4 Color in each "slice" with a differently colored felt-tipped pen. Remember to follow the order of colors in the rainbow spectrum: red, orange, yellow, green, blue, indigo and violet.

5 Push the skewer through the center of the cardboard disc, where the compass point was, to make a spinning top. You may need help with this. Attach the skewer firmly to the disc with small blobs of modeling clay.

6 Spin the disc like a top, by rolling the skewer very fast between your finger and thumb. You may need some practice to make this work properly.

## Mixing Beams

If you mixed together the ink from the colored pens you have used for your rainbow on a piece of paper, it would make a purple-brown mess. So why do the spinning colors seem to look white?

It is because when you spin the disc, it is not the inks of the pens that are mixing together. Instead, it is the colored light beams, which are bouncing off each colored "slice," that are mixing together.

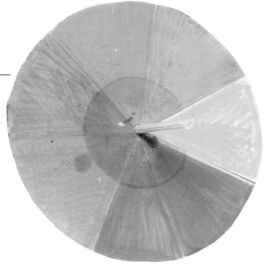

# Magical Magic Markers

When you paint a picture, do you mix lots of colors to make the exact shade of color you need? You can make hundreds of different colors, even if you only have a few paints to start with. In fact, you need only three colors to make any other color you want. These colors are red, blue and yellow. They are called the primary colors. You can make any other color by mixing them, but you cannot make a primary color by mixing any other colors. Antonino is finding out which colors of inks were mixed to make the colors of his felt-tipped pens.

## Real science

In science, this experiment is called **chromatography**. It works because, the water creeps up the blotting paper, it carries with it the different colored inks at different speeds. Chromatography is very important science. It is used by scientists to separate all sorts of mixtures a combinations, like salty sea water or a piece of moon rock, to find out what is really in them.

YOU WILL NEED THESE
MATERIALS AND TOOLS

White blotting paper

Scissors

Water-soluble, felt-tipped pens in several different colors

Jars

Water

Antonino shows that his red, yellow and blue felt-tipped pens are not what they seem. They contain mixtures of inks of different colors.

## Your Science Record Book

Let the strips of blotting paper dry on a newspaper, and stick them in your Science Record Book. Write the color of the felt-tipped pen you used on each strip of blotting paper, using a pencil (which is not affected by water) or by marking them with the original pen right at the top. The bands of colors on the blotting paper show the separate ink colors that were mixed together to make the color of that pen. If the felt-tipped pen was orange, green, purple or brown, there are probably lots of color bands. If the pen was one of the primary colors – red, blue or yellow – there may be only one or two bands.

1 Carefully cut the blotting paper into long strips that will fit inside the jars. Make a large ink blot about ¼ in from one edge of each piece of blotting paper with a differently colored felt-tipped pen.

2 Allow the blots to dry thoroughly. Stand each piece of blotting paper in a jar with the blot toward the bottom of the jar.

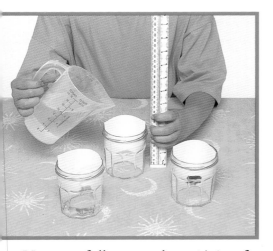

3 Very carefully pour about ½ in of water into each jar. Do not let the level of the water reach the ink blots, and try not to splash the blotting paper as you pour.

4 Check the jars every few minutes. You will see the water being soaked up by the blotting paper. When the water gets near to the top, take the blotting paper out of the jars.

This is a fairly straightforward experiment but it might be a little messy, so cover surfaces with newspaper or provide a waterproof area. The experiment takes time to work, perhaps a few hours. But the results are clearest if the inks are not left too long, otherwise they get drawn to the edge of the paper and combine again.

19

# Balloon Snowstorm

Electricity is strange stuff. It is invisible, which means we cannot see it. But it is also very powerful, and it can be very dangerous. We use electricity in our homes in lots of different ways to make things work, such as light bulbs, heaters, vacuum cleaners, washing machines, radios and music players. This electricity is very strong. NEVER go near this electricity. However, you can make your own electricity, which is safe and fun. It does not move along wires, and it is not as powerful as electricity that runs through wires. It is called static electricity.

Lorenzo has charged his balloon with static electricity by rubbing it against his T-shirt. Now, the tissue-paper "snow flakes" stick to it.

## YOU WILL NEED THESE MATERIALS AND TOOLS

Balloons

Scissors

Tissue paper

Wear a cotton T-shirt or woolen sweater

## Charge your balloon

Tiny bits of static electricity are called charges. These can be **positive** or **negative,** just like the two connections on a battery. (See the experiment called Battery Light Show.) An object such as a balloon has an equal number of positive and negative charges over its surface. They cancel each other out, so over a whole balloon, there is no static electricity. But when a balloon is rubbed against a different material, such as a T-shirt, some of the positive charges go on to the T-shirt and stay there. This leaves extra negative charges on the balloon, which make it "sticky."

⚠️ Making static electricity is easier on cold, dry days. On warm, humid days, the air itself is full of static. Children might need help blowing up and tying balloons.

1 Blow up a balloon, and tie the neck. Do not blow your balloon up too much that it bursts, but make sure it is fairly hard, since a soft, squashy balloon does not work so well.

2 Make some "snow" by tearing or cutting tissue paper into little bits. If you have the time, you could make each "flake" a pointed star with six sides, like real snow flakes.

3 Rub the balloon several times on your T-shirt or woolly sweater. Rub it real fast until the balloon "sticks" to the T-shirt or sweater. The balloon is now charged with static electricity.

4 Hold the balloon near the "snow." The flakes are lifted up by the static electricity on the balloon. After a little while, the electricity leaks away, and the flakes fall softly.

5 Rub your balloon again to re-charge it. Then hold it near a friend's hair and see what happens. For the best effect, choose someone with long hair.

## Push and Pull

There are two types of static-electricity charges, positive and negative. Charges which are different **attract** or pull each other together. So the balloon sticks to anything with the opposite charge, even water. Lorenzo is holding a charged balloon near a stream of water. It should attract the water and bend the stream toward it. Charges which are the same **repel**, or push each other away. So the balloon pushes away anything with the same charge as itself, such as another charged balloon. Write or draw what happens in your Science Record Book when you try these experiments.

# Battery Light Show

Kirsty has made a light show to demonstrate how electricity works. Electricity is stored in the battery. It can only move, or flow, when it has a complete circle or circuit to go around. This circuit is made from wires, a switch and a bulb. When the switch is ON, the electricity goes from one end, or terminal, on the battery, along the wires, through the switch and light bulb, back to the battery's other terminal. As electricity goes through the bulb, it glows. When the switch is OFF, it makes a gap or break in the circuit. The electricity stops, and the light goes out.

### Electric likes and dislikes

Electricity flows easily through some materials, like metals such as steel, iron and copper and also, water. These are called **conductors**. Electricity cannot flow through other things, like plastic, wood and pottery. These are called **insulators**. The wires in this experiment are made of metal on the inside, so the electricity can flow. The wire is covered with plastic to stop the electricity from escaping.

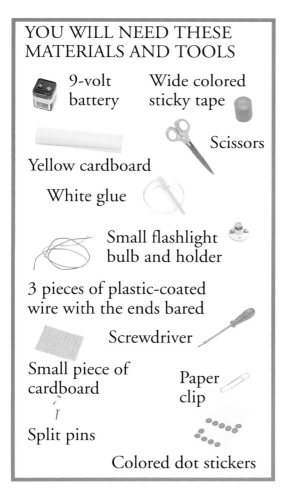

## YOU WILL NEED THESE MATERIALS AND TOOLS

- 9-volt battery
- Wide colored sticky tape
- Scissors
- Yellow cardboard
- White glue
- Small flashlight bulb and holder
- 3 pieces of plastic-coated wire with the ends bared
- Screwdriver
- Small piece of cardboard
- Paper clip
- Split pins
- Colored dot stickers

⚠ A 9-volt battery is perfectly safe for doing experiments. A grown-up should strip about ¹/₂ in of plastic from both ends of each piece of wire. Be careful how you screw the light bulb into its holder, since too much force may break the glass. Young children might need help with screws and screwdrivers.

**WARNING**

NEVER TOUCH ELECTRICAL WIRES, SWITCHES, PLUGS OR SOCKETS WITHOUT HELP FROM A GROWN-UP.

Kirsty switches the light on and off, showing how she can start and stop the electricity going through the circuit.

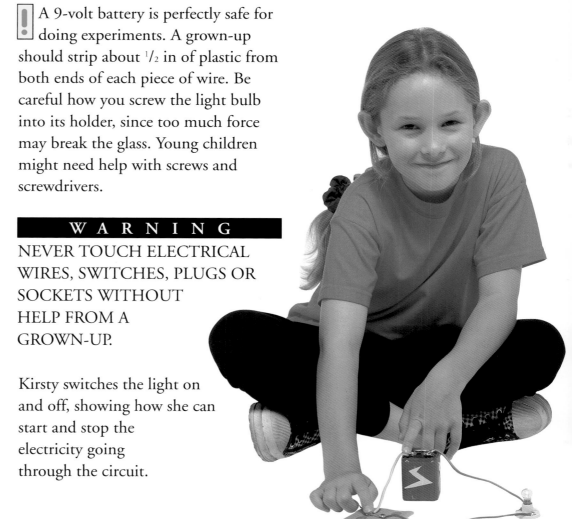

1 Decorate the battery to make it look powerful by winding a piece f wide colored sticky tape around it.

2 Cut out some zigzag "lightning flashes" from the yellow cardboard and stick them on to the sides of the battery with glue.

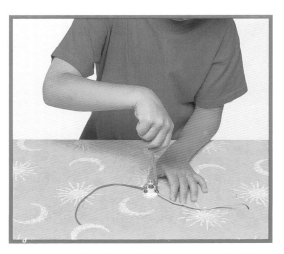

3 Screw the light bulb into the holder. Push the end of a piece of wire under one of the connecting screws. Screw it down. Repeat with another piece of wire under the other screw.

4 Take the end of one of these pieces of wire and twist it on to one of he battery terminals (the bits of metal n the top of the battery).

5 Twist the end of the third piece of wire on to the other battery terminal. Make sure that both these wires grip the terminals tightly.

7 Twist one free wire end around one split pin and the other around the other split pin. When the paper clip touches both split pins, the switch is ON (green dot) and the light bulb shines. When the paper clip is moved away from the split pin, the switch is OFF (red dot).

6 Push two holes through the piece of cardboard, the length of the paper clip apart. Push a split pin through one hole. Push the other split pin through the paper clip and then through the other hole. Open the ends of the pins under the card.

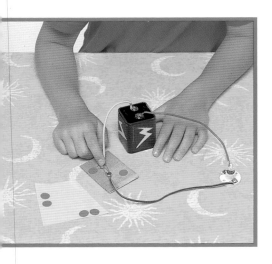

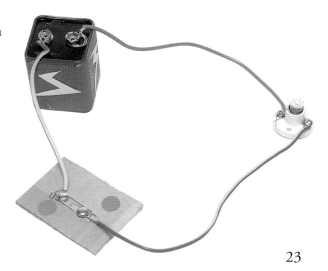

# Sound Cannon

Sound is caused by very fast to-and-fro movements in the air, called **vibrations**. When something makes a sound, invisible ripples or vibrations spread out through the air, like ripples in a pond, to your ears. These are called sound waves. The bigger the vibrations, the louder the sound. In this experiment, Liam shouts loudly into the sound cannon, to make the plastic sheet vibrate inside it. This vibrates the air inside the cannon. The sound waves come out of the hole at the end with such force that they knock over the bowling pins.

Liam is trying to knock all the bowling pins over with one blast of sound waves from his sound cannon.

## Play a game

Stand your "bowling" pins in rows like in a ten-pin bowling alley – one in front, two behind, then three, and so on. Point the cannon at the pins with the hole toward them. You can shout a the stretched plastic sheet of your cannon, or tap it with your fingers. How many pins can you knock down with one try? You can play a game with a friend. Hold the cannon behind a line and give three shouts each.

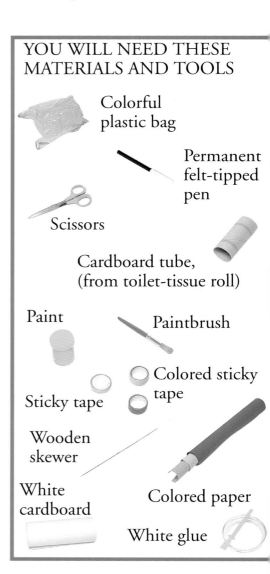

YOU WILL NEED THESE MATERIALS AND TOOLS

Colorful plastic bag

Permanent felt-tipped pen

Scissors

Cardboard tube, (from toilet-tissue roll)

Paint

Paintbrush

Sticky tape

Colored sticky tape

Wooden skewer

White cardboard

Colored paper

White glue

! The plastic sheets of the cannon must be tight, so a child might need help with stretching and sticking them. A grown-up should make the hole in the plastic sheet with a sharp point. The louder, shorter and sharper the sound used, the better the result.

1 Draw two circles on the plastic bag about twice as big as the ends of the cardboard tube. Use another object as a guide. Use a permanent felt-tipped pen for this. Cut out the circles.

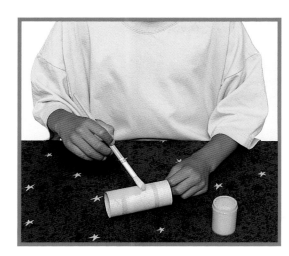

2 Paint the cardboard tube in a bright color. You may need two coats of paint for a good effect. Allow to dry.

3 Place the plastic circles tightly over the ends of the tube. You might need someone to help stretch the plastic tight while you stick it with sticky tape.

4 Decorate the tube by winding colored sticky tape around it to make stripes.

5 Ask a grown-up to help you make a tiny hole with a skewer in the center of one stretched plastic sheet at one end of the cannon.

6 Draw some bowling-pin shapes on the white cardboard. Cut out the pins. Leave an extra bit on the bottom of each as a "foot."

7 Decorate your pins with strips of colored paper and sticky tape. Glue the paper on to the pins.

8 Trim the colored paper strips to the same shape as the pins with scissors. Bend the "feet" toward you.

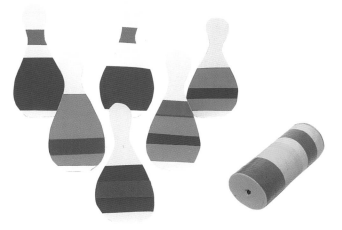

25

# Tumbler Telephone

Can you talk to a friend quietly, when he or she is at the other end of a big room? Liam's telephone works by sending the sound waves of his voice along the string. They go along the string as very fast to-and-fro movements called vibrations. When Liam talks into the tumbler or cup, the sound waves hit the bottom of the tumbler and make it vibrate.

The vibrations pass along the string to the tumbler at the other end. They shake the bottom of this tumbler, which makes sound waves that go into Lorenzo's ear.

With his own tumbler telephone, Liam never gets a wrong number, and the lines are never busy. Also, his calls are always free!

## Traveling waves

Sound waves travel well through air. They go through lots of other things too, such as water, wood, metals and glass. In fact, sound travels much faster and further as vibrations in water, metal and glass than it does through air. This is why whales and dolphins can "talk" to each other across huge distances in the ocean.

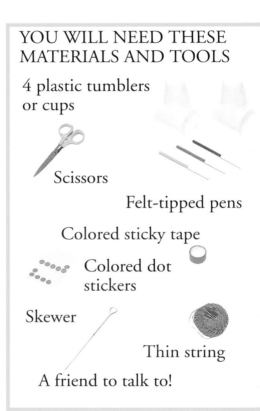

YOU WILL NEED THESE
MATERIALS AND TOOLS

4 plastic tumblers
or cups

Scissors

Felt-tipped pens

Colored sticky tape

Colored dot
stickers

Skewer

Thin string

A friend to talk to!

The tumbler telephone works well i the string is stretched tight and straight, and nothing touches it. Otherwise the vibrations cannot trave along it properly. The tumblers should be held by their rims only, so the bottoms are free to vibrate. Children may need help with cutting the tumblers and making holes with a sharp point.

Carefully cut the bottoms off two of the tumblers about ³/₄ in from the base. You may need to ask a grown-up to help you with this.

2 Stick the top of a felt-tipped pen to the bottom of each of the other two tumblers. These will be the "antennas."

3 Ask a grown-up to cut small holes in the cut-off tumbler bottoms. Slip them neatly over the "antennas" to hold them in place.

4 Tape the cut-off bottoms in place. Add more strips of sticky tape for decoration.

5 Make a "key pad" on each telephone with colored dot stickers. Write numbers on the dots.

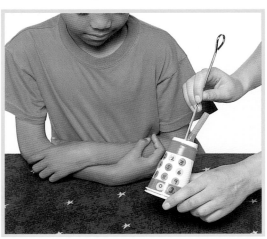

6 Ask a grown-up to make a tiny hole in the bottoms of the tumblers with a skewer.

7 Thread the ends of the string through the holes in the telephones. Tie a large knot in each end of the string.

# Chatting on the Telephone

Your friend walks away with one of the tumbler telephones, until the string is stretched tight, and holds the telephone to his or her ear. You speak into the telephone, and your friend listens. When you have finished talking, say "Over" like a real walkie-talkie user. Hold the telephone to your ear to hear your friend's reply. Try using longer string to see if the telephone still works. Measure the greatest length, and write the results in your Science Record Book.

27

# Marvelous Mobiles

Air is all around us. We cannot see it or touch it. But when it moves, we can feel it. Moving air comes from your mouth when you blow, and from a fan. The wind is moving air. Stand outside on a windy day, and sometimes, the moving air nearly knocks you over. Antonino's marvelous mobile swirls and twirls when moving air pushes it. You can find moving air around the house, such as near a window, door, radiator or table lamp.

## Rising air

Indoors, moving air is sometimes called a draft, especially when it is cold and unwanted. Drafts in houses are caused by the wind blowing through gaps around windows or doors. Drafts are also caused in other ways. Hot air from a radiator or table lamp rises up to the ceiling and makes a warm draft. On a cold night, cold air near a window fall to the floor as a cold draft.

Children may need help with cutting and balancing the mobile. Hanging the mobile near any heat source, such as a radiator or lamp, must be supervised.

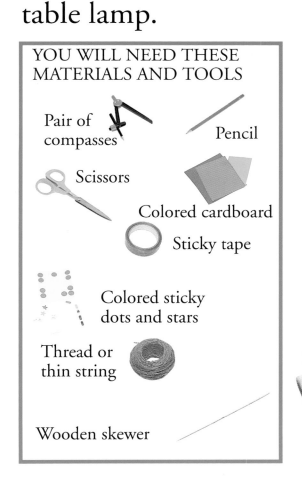

YOU WILL NEED THESE
MATERIALS AND TOOLS

Pair of compasses

Pencil

Scissors

Colored cardboard

Sticky tape

Colored sticky dots and stars

Thread or thin string

Wooden skewer

Antonino can use his marvelous mobile to detect wind, drafts and other moving air in his house.

1 Use the compasses to draw lots of circles on the colored cardboard. Make them any size but there must be two of each size.

2 Carefully cut out the circles using scissors. Arrange the discs in their equal-sized pairs.

3 Carefully cut a straight line or slit from the edge of each disc to its center, where the compass point was.

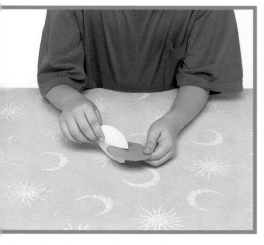

4 Push the two discs of each pair together by their slits. Secure the seams with some sticky tape to make sure they hold together.

5 Decorate the discs with the colored dots and stars.

6 Cut the string or thread into different lengths. Stick one end of a string to the center of each pair of discs. Tie the other end to the skewer.

## A Mobile Draft Detector

Balance the mobile by moving the strings along the skewer until it does not tip over. Now, find places around the house where you can hang the mobile. If it turns or wobbles, you know there is air moving past it. Make a list of the places you test in your Science Record Book. Can you think what might cause the drafts?

*Above:* Tie another length of string to the center of the skewer so you can hang it up.

# Super Sailboat

When air moves outside, it is called wind. Wind can be very powerful. Strong winds, called gales, blow down trees and damage buildings. People have used the power of the wind for thousands of years to push the sails of their boats and travel across lakes, rivers and seas. Dean is going sailing, too, with his super sailboat. You can make it move by producing your own wind as you blow into the sail. Or you can sail it outdoors on a breezy day.

Young children may need help cutting the plastic tumbler. A grown-up should push the skewer into the "boat." Outdoor sailing must always be supervised.

Dean blows his super sailboat across the "sea" to demonstrate the power of the wind.

## Super sailors

The Ancient Egyptians, who built the Great Pyramids, discovered how to sail boats more than five-thousand years ago. As people learned more about sailing, they built bigger ships with more sails. Some great sailing ships had more than thirty sails! Today, most big ships are powered by engines that turn propellers. But many people still enjoy the sport of sailing.

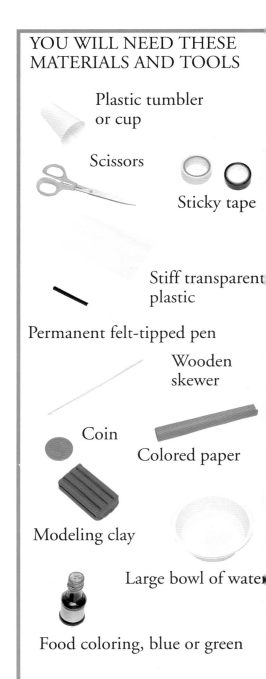

YOU WILL NEED THESE MATERIALS AND TOOLS

Plastic tumbler or cup

Scissors

Sticky tape

Stiff transparent plastic

Permanent felt-tipped pen

Wooden skewer

Coin

Colored paper

Modeling clay

Large bowl of water

Food coloring, blue or green

1 Carefully cut an oval hole in the side of a plastic cup. You can cut through the rim. You may need to ask a grown-up to help with this.

2 Repair the cut rim, and make the boat stronger at the same time, by putting two or three layers of sticky tape all around the rim.

3 Draw around the rim of the cup on to the transparent plastic. Use a permanent felt-tipped pen for this. Ordinary felt-tip ink may rub off.

4 Cut out the circle. Tape it firmly over the rim of the cup to make the back end of your boat.

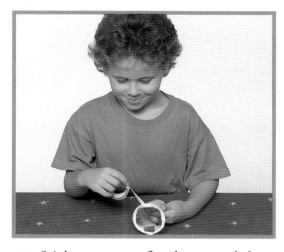

5 Stick extra tape firmly around the rim of the cup. This makes sure the boat will not leak.

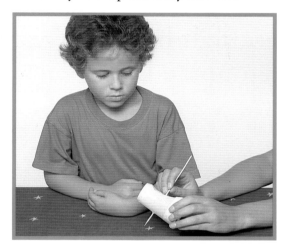

6 Ask a grown-up to push the skewer through the bottom of the boat. It is both the mast above the boat and the keel underneath in the water.

## Sailing Forward, and Sideways

The sail works best if it is slightly curled, like Dean's. The coin on the keel will keep the boat upright. When you blow on the boat, which way does the sail turn to catch the wind? Make the boat go straight across the water to the other side. Can you make the boat go sideways? Try twisting the sail around on the mast. This will make the boat go in a different direction.

7 Cut a sail from colored paper. Ask a grown-up to make two holes in it, top and bottom, and thread it on to the skewer mast. Tape a coin to the keel with sticky tape.

8 Push the skewer up, so the coin is against the bottom. Secure it in place with modeling clay. Add some blue or green food coloring to the water or "sea" in the bowl.

# Hold Water Upside Down!

This famous trick looks impossible, or perhaps it is magic. Can you really hold water in an upside-down tumbler? Yes. Antonino shows that it truly does work. It depends on science. The force that pulls you, a cat, a chair and everything else in the world, down toward the ground is called gravity. Gravity tries to make the water fall out of the upside-down tumbler toward the ground. But in this trick, air keeps the water in the tumbler.

## Heavy air

Air has weight, although it does not weigh much. There is a lot of it pressing on us, since there is a huge amount of air high above. We do not notice this pressing force, because we are used to it. It is called **air pressure**, and it is this that keeps the water in the glass. The water is trapped inside the glass by the cardboard. Air presses down, around and up underneath the cardboard, holding it in place and keeping the water inside the tumbler.

## YOU WILL NEED THESE MATERIALS AND TOOLS

Large bowl of water

Food coloring

Plastic tumbler

Pencil

Thick, smooth, shiny, flat cardboard

Scissors

❗ This experiment involves a lot of water and does not always work right the first time. So it should be performed in a suitable waterproof area. Use a plastic tumbler and bowl rather than glass ones, for safety. We have used glass ones here so you can see how the experiment works. Clean, smooth, shiny, flat cardboard is best. The experiment does not work as well if the cardboard becomes soggy or bent.

Antonino is using the science of air, water and gravity to stop his feet from getting wet!

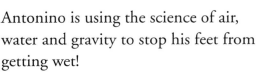

1 Add a little food coloring to the water in the bowl, and stir it round. This is so you can see the water inside the tumbler.

2 Draw around the rim of the tumbler on to the cardboard. Then draw a square around this circle, about ³/₄ in larger than the circle all around.

3 Carefully cut out the square of cardboard. It should fit easily over the top of the tumbler, with plenty of extra around the rim.

4 Put the tumbler into the bowl of water. Hold it under, with the open end pointing up. Make sure that it fills up completely.

5 Make sure there are no bubbles of air inside the tumbler, by tapping it. The trick will not work if there is any air in the tumbler.

6 Turn the tumbler upside down. Lift it partly out, but keep the rim under the water. Slide the cardboard into the water and under the rim.

7 Hold the cardboard firmly against the rim of the tumbler. Slowly lift the cardboard and tumbler, still upside down, out of the water.

8 Hold the tumbler upside down and level. Without sliding the cardboard, take your other hand away from the cardboard.

## Air, Water and Weather

The layer of air all around the Earth is called the **atmosphere**. Air's weight changes when it gets hot or cold, and these changes cause our weather. When air is warmed by the sun, it rises higher. Cooler air moves along to take its place. This is wind. As air rises, the invisible moisture in it turns to tiny drops of water. These make clouds. As the drops get bigger, they fall as rain.

# Sink or Swim

Water is very strong. It can push things. When it flows in rivers, or in sea currents, it pushes objects along. Water also pushes down all the time, because it is very heavy. But it also pushes up, too. This upward pushing is called upthrust, and it makes things float. Izabella is discovering that water's upthrust is strong enough to support some things and make them float, but that others are too heavy and sink.

## Floating forces

An object floats if the upward push of the water, called **upthrust,** is more than the downward push of the object. The downward push of the object is called **displacement** because it moves aside (dis-places) some water. An object that is small for its weight, like a pebble, displaces only a small amount of water. So it sinks. If an object is large for its weight, like a sponge, it floats.

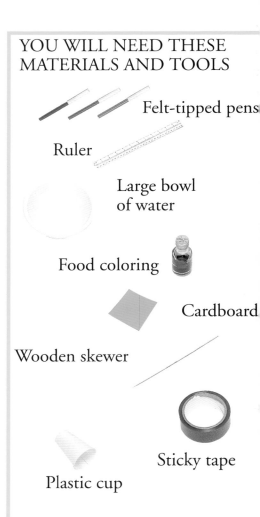

YOU WILL NEED THESE
MATERIALS AND TOOLS

Felt-tipped pens

Ruler

Large bowl
of water

Food coloring

Cardboard

Wooden skewer

Sticky tape

Plastic cup

Household items or toys like a cork, pumice stone, pebble, small strainer, metal dish, clothespin, dry sponge, paper clip, wooden spoon, metal spoon, nail, piece of polystyrene, table-tennis ball

! Do not use glass or sharp objects in this experiment. A suitable waterproof area is essential.

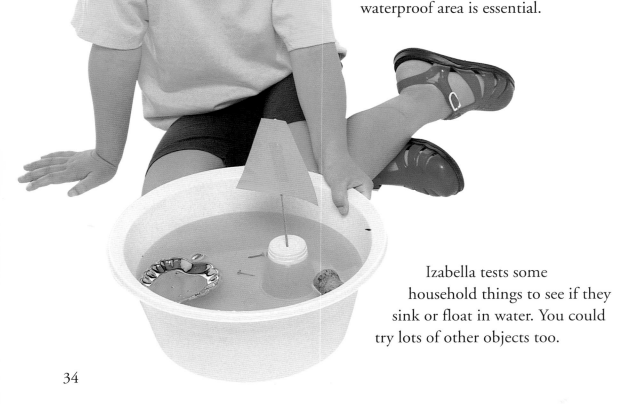

Izabella tests some household things to see if they sink or float in water. You could try lots of other objects too.

1 Draw a chart in your Science Record Book with three columns. In the first column, write the names or draw the items you will test. The middle column is for those that SWIM. The last is for those that SINK.

2 Ask a grown-up to fill a large bowl of water. Stir in some food coloring – just for fun!

3 Make a floating marker by cutting out a sail shape from the piece of cardboard. Tape it to a wooden skewer. Ask a grown-up to push the skewer into the bottom of a plastic cup. Half fill the cup with water, and float it.

4 Put the cork, the pumice stone and the pebble on the surface of the water. Do they sink or swim?

5 Put a cross in the SINK or a check mark in the SWIM column of your Science Record Book for each item.

6 Try to float the small strainer and the metal dish. Put the results in your Science Record Book.

7 Test a clothespin and the sponge. Leave the sponge in the water for a long time. Does it still float as high?

# Weight, Shape and Water

If something has air in it, like the dry sponge, it weighs less. So it is likely to float. The metal dish also has air "in" it when it is right side up, so it floats, too. This is how metal boats float. If the air is replaced by water, the object becomes heavier, and it may sink. This is why the sponge gradually floats lower as it soaks up water. Tip over the dish, and it fills with water and sinks. This is what happens when a boat capsizes. The floating marker is half full of water and half full of air, so it half floats. Pumice stone is bubbly rock full of air that is made by volcanoes.

35

# The Great Iceberg Puzzle

One of the great puzzles of nature is how icebergs float. Icebergs are huge lumps of ice that drift about in the cold seas near the North and South Poles. Some icebergs are bigger than cities. They weigh thousands of tons. As water gets colder, it gets heavier. So cold water sinks below warm water. Icebergs are frozen water and so are even colder. So why do they not sink to the bottom of the sea? Lorenzo finds out why in this experiment by using tiny icebergs from a refrigerator or freezer. They will work the same as a real iceberg, but they are much smaller!

Lorenzo has made lots of colored "icebergs." He is investigating how they float and then melt.

## YOU WILL NEED THESE MATERIALS AND TOOLS

A large see-through bowl of warm water

Ice-cube tray

Food colorings

Pitcher

Plastic paint pots or jars

Spoon

## Light ice

As water gets colder, it becomes heavier. But this only happens down to the temperature of 4°C (40°F). If it gets colder than that, it begins to get lighter again and so rises toward the surface. When it cools to 0°C (32°F), liquid water freezes into solid ice. This cold ice is light, and it floats on water. This means that animals and plants which live in water do not have to freeze solid themselves when the temperature drops to or below freezing. They can survive in the cold water below the ice that floats on ponds and lakes.

1 Make some mini-icebergs by putting food coloring into some water in paint pots or jars. You can make them in several different colors, but do not mix the colors together.

2 Spoon the colored water carefully into the ice-cube tray or other containers, if you wish. Put these into a freezer. Leave until frozen solid.

3 When the ice cubes are frozen, fill the large bowl with warm water. Ask a grown-up to help you with this. Then remove the ice-cube tray from the freezer or refrigerator.

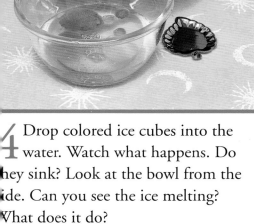

4 Drop colored ice cubes into the water. Watch what happens. Do they sink? Look at the bowl from the side. Can you see the ice melting? What does it do?

This experiment needs a waterproof area. Young children will need help with warm water and with the bowl, especially if it is glass. Handle ice with care since it can stick to the skin and "burns" with intense cold. Dip the ice-cube tray in water to prevent this and to free the cubes. Also, use of the freezer must always be supervised.

## Underwater Fountain

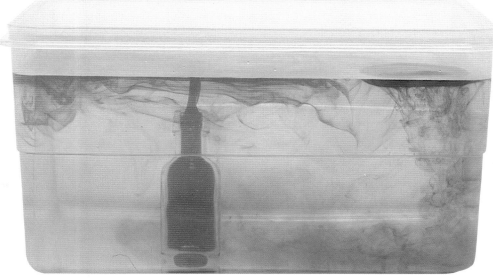

You can investigate how warm water floats and cold water sinks by making an underwater fountain. Fill a large bowl with cold water. Then fill a small plastic bottle with warm water. (The plastic bottle must be small enough to sink below the surface of the water in the bowl.) Add some food coloring to it. Carefully lower the bottle into the bowl, and make it sit on the bottom. Does the warm, colored water stay in the bottle? Where does it go? Draw a picture of your fountain in your Science Research Book to show your results. You could also try dropping some colored ice cubes, made with a contrasting food coloring, into the water. The ice is lighter than the water around it, so it floats. The warmer water melts the colored ice. But the colored water that comes from the ice is colder and heavier than the water around it, so it sinks. Look very carefully to see the cold, colored water trickling from the iceberg and sinking to the bottom.

# Kitchen Chemistry

Everything in the world is made of chemicals. Some are artificial chemicals, like those made in factories. Others are natural chemicals, like those in your own body and in the rocks and soil. Even the food you eat is made of chemicals. Scientists who study chemicals are called chemists. You can be a kitchen chemist, like Dean, and study the chemicals in the cabinet. Cooking is a form of chemistry. You mix together the chemicals and make them join together, or react, to form a tasty snack.

## The acid test

Some cooking substances, like vinegar or lemon juice, are sour. They are called **acidic**. Other kitchen substance like baking soda, are slightly slimy and bitter. They are called **basic** or **alkali**. Bases are the opposite of acids. Chemists often need to know whether chemicals are acids or bases. If they do not know what the chemicals are, they should never taste them to find out, because many chemicals are poisonous So chemists make special substances called **chemical indicators** to test them Red cabbage water is a good chemical indicator to tell the difference between acids and bases.

! Young children must be supervised in the kitchen since some foods and liquids can cause sickness in large quantities. Chopping and boiling the cabbage should always be done by a grown-up.

Dean has put a strip of blotting paper into each of his test jars. The name of the test juice or liquid is marked on the paper in pencil. He can then let the strips dry and clip them into his Science Record Book.

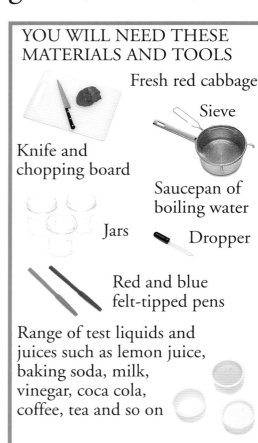

YOU WILL NEED THESE MATERIALS AND TOOLS

Fresh red cabbage

Sieve

Knife and chopping board

Saucepan of boiling water

Jars

Dropper

Red and blue felt-tipped pens

Range of test liquids and juices such as lemon juice, baking soda, milk, vinegar, coca cola, coffee, tea and so on

1 Ask a grown-up to chop the cabbage, put it into boiling water for about 15 minutes, then strain the water through a sieve.

2 While the chemical indicator (the red cabbage water) is cooling, put a little tap water into each jar. Get your Science Record Book ready.

3 Add about 15 drops of the chemical indicator to each jar, using the dropper. Look at the color and note it in your Science Record Book.

4 Add one test liquid to a jar, such as a spoonful of juice squeezed from lemon. Stir it in. Watch and note down any color change.

5 Add another test liquid, such as a spoonful of milk, to the next jar. As before, mix it, and note down any color change in your book.

6 Add the next test liquid, such as a few drops of vinegar, to the next jar. Note any change. Do this with the other test liquids and juices.

# Recording Your Results

Color in the result of each experiment in your Science Record Book. Draw three columns. In the first column, write the name or draw a picture of the test substance. In the second column, put a check mark for those that turned red or orange with a red felt-tipped pen. In the third column, put a check mark for those that turned purple or blue with a blue felt-tipped pen. Acids join or react with the red cabbage water to turn it red or orange. Bases do the same but turn it purple or blue. During the experiment, keep one jar that contains just the chemical indicator. Scientists call this a "control." You can compare the color changes in the other jars with the original color in the "control" jar.

# Vinegar Volcano

What happens when acids and bases (alkalis) meet? Kirsty has made a peaceful-looking tropical island, but it is about to get shaken by a huge volcano. She can make the volcano explode or erupt using simple chemicals – the acid vinegar and the base bicarbonate of soda. The spectacular effect is caused by the reaction between the acid and the base. The food coloring makes it look like real, red-hot, runny rock.

## YOU WILL NEED THESE MATERIALS AND TOOLS

Red food coloring

Vinegar

2 small plastic or glass bottles

Funnel

Baking soda

Large, blue plate

Sand

White glue

Colored paper

Pencil

Scissors

Colored sticky tape

## Fizzy gas

Everything is made of chemicals. And all chemicals are made of tiny particles called **atoms**. During a chemical reaction, the groups of atoms are taken apart, mixed and shuffled, then joined together in different groups, to make new chemicals. When vinegar is mixed with baking soda, one of the new chemicals formed is a gas. The bubbles of this gas make the volcano fizz.

This chemical reaction is not dangerous. The gas produced is carbon dioxide, but with the recommended quantities of vinegar and baking soda, its amounts are very small and not harmful. However, the child should be supervised in case of spillage.

Kirsty's volcano is based on a simple chemical reaction. A real volcano is millions of times more powerful and based on heat and pressure.

1 Add some red food coloring to some vinegar in a small bottle using the funnel.

2 Wash and dry the funnel. Use it to put 3 or 4 teaspoons of baking soda into another small bottle.

3 Stand this bottle in the middle of the plate as the volcano. Pile the sand around it.

4 Paint the sides of the bottle with glue, to make the sand stick. Leave the bottle's mouth clear. This is the volcano's opening or crater.

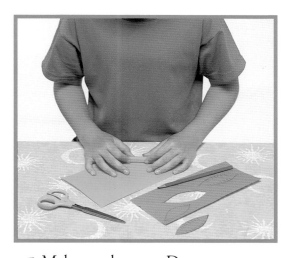

5 Make a palm tree. Draw some leaves on green paper, and cut them out. Snip around their edges to make fronds. Roll up some colored paper to make the tree trunk.

6 Tape round the top and bottom of the trunk, and cut it off square, so it stands up. Tape the palm leaf shapes to the top of the trunk.

7 Using the funnel, carefully pour some of the colored vinegar on to the bicarb in the bottle on the island, and quickly remove the funnel.

## Lots of Eruptions

The red, bubbly "lava" fizzes out of the top of the volcano. The chemical reaction starts as soon as the vinegar mixes with the baking soda. When the volcano has finished erupting, stir inside the bottle with a skewer and pour in some more vinegar. You may get several eruptions this way.

41